CW01091192

LOVE AND MARRIAGE

LOVE AND MARRIAGE

Anne Townsend

Illustrated by
LUCINDA ROGERS

COLLINS
8 Grafton Street, London W1
1989

William Collins Sons & Co. Ltd
London · Glasgow · Sydney · Auckland
Toronto · Johannesburg

First published 1989
© Anne Townsend 1989
Illustrations © Collins
Publishers PLC, 1989

ISBN 0-00-215536-2

Set in Linotron Palatino by
Rowland Phototypesetting Ltd
Bury St Edmunds, Suffolk
Printed and Bound in Great Britain by
T. J. Press (Padstow) Ltd, Padstow, Cornwall

CONTENTS

LOVE AND MARRIAGE

PART THREE *The Later Years*

For John,
my partner for nearly three decades,
with love . . .

PART ONE

Falling in Love

1 ~ HEAD OVER HEELS

In today's Western culture the phenomenon described as "falling in love" is usually a prerequisite to marriage. This peculiar state of mind is displayed in various ways – all of which emphasize the existence of a remarkably high degree of blissful disregard of objective reality about the two individuals concerned.

"We were engaged . . ."

It is not easy to describe goodness; it usually comes out smug, unadventurous and without humour or warmth. I have always wanted to write a story or a play about goodness, because, when I meet it, it has always attracted me more than anything else. But it is hard to put on paper. The goodness I mean is a sense of unchanging security, in the widest sense of wholeness; and it is never suspected by those who have it. In it their natural essence, their being expresses it, not in words, but in attitudes and behaviour.

1

I have met a lot of it, in a variety of people, but nowhere more consistently than in Reggie . . . But I don't know how to write about it without outlining, and the point about goodness is that it cannot be confined or described, it can only be sensed or experienced in a relationship. It is one of the highest expressions of love – not as A loves B, but as love makes the world go round in a far wider context.

JOYCE GRENFELL

Contradictions Fall

The word "falling" in the phrase "falling in love" is a contra-diction in itself. Since loving is a productive activity, one can only *stand* in love or *walk* in love: one cannot "fall" in love, for falling denotes passivity.

ERICH FROMM

2 ~ FROM THE SUBLIME . . .

One of love's great bonuses is that it inspires a high degree of self-giving in the partners.

Bridal Love

. . . married love . . . is a bridal love that burns like fire and seeks nothing else but the married partner. It says: I do not want what is yours, I want neither silver nor gold, neither this nor that; I want only you yourself; I want it all or nothing. All other love seeks something other than the one it loves; this love alone wants the beloved himself. And if Adam had not fallen, the loveliest of all things would have been bride and bridegroom.

MARTIN LUTHER

Transforming Love

There is no way under the sun to make a man worthy of love except by loving him. As soon as he realizes himself loved – if he is not so weak that he can no longer bear to be loved – he will feel himself instantly becoming worthy of love. He will respond by drawing a mysterious spiritual value out of his own depths, a new identity called into being by the love that is addressed to him.

THOMAS MERTON

The Fourth Mystery

Three things there are too wonderful for me,
Four which I do not comprehend:
The way of an eagle in the air,
The way of a snake on a rock,
The way of a ship in the midst of the sea,
And the way of a man with a maid.

Proverbs 30:18–19

3

Love Is Created Every Day

Love does not just happen; it is created through decisions we make, the give and take of day-to-day relationships, and by reflection, listening, and knowing ourselves . . . our strengths and weaknesses.

CHUCK GALLAGHER, S.J.

Priorities

In marriage do thou be wise: prefer the person before the money, virtue before beauty, the mind before the body; then thou hast a wife, a friend, a companion, a second self.

WILLIAM PENN

Yours

The life that I have is all that I have,
   The life that I have is yours.

The love that I have of the life that I have,
   Is yours and yours and yours.

A sleep I shall have, a rest I shall have,
   Yet death will be but a pause.

For the peace of my years in the long green grass
   Will be yours and yours and yours.

VIOLETTE SZABO

3 . . . TO THE RIDICULOUS

Love may be so blind to reality that absurd situations arise . . .

Reasonable Reason?

The first need of most men in our society is practical. They have not been taught how to cook and mend and sew. There is no reason why boys are unable to learn these things, but generally they are not taught, for it is assumed they will marry and their wives will do these things for them. If they have been rendered unable to look after themselves, this is a very good reason why they do indeed need a wife.

TONY WALTER

Blind But . . .

Maybe you heard about the man who fell in love with an opera singer. He hardly knew her, since his only view of the singer was through binoculars – from the third balcony. But he was convinced that he could live "happy ever after" married to a voice like that. He scarcely noticed she was considerably older than he. Nor did he care that she walked with a limp. Her mezzo-soprano voice would take them through whatever might come. After a whirlwind romance and a hurry-up ceremony, they were off for their honeymoon together.

She began to prepare for their first night together. As he watched, his chin dropped to his chest. She plucked out her glass eye and plopped it into a container on the bedside table. She pulled off her wig, ripped off her false eyelashes, yanked out her false teeth, unstrapped her artificial leg, and smiled at him as she slipped off the glasses that hid her hearing aid. Stunned and horrified, he gasped, "For goodness sake, woman, sing, sing, SING!"

CHARLES SWINDOLL

Computer Love

> I love your eyes, your cherry lips,
> the love that always lingers,
> your way with words and random blibs,
> your skilled computer fingers.

ALVIN TOFFLER

Gain Not Loss

There was a famous story about how a man once said to Rabbi Gamaliel: "Your God is a thief because it is written, The Lord God caused a deep sleep to fall upon Adam, and he slept; and he took one of his ribs" (Genesis 2:21). The rabbi's daughter said to her father, "Leave him to me; I will answer him." She

then said to the man, "Give me an officer to investigate a complaint." "For what purpose?" he said. She replied, "Thieves broke into our house during the night and stole a silver ewer belonging to us, but left a gold one behind." The man exclaimed, "Would that such a thief visited me every day!" She answered, "Was it not then a splendid thing for the first man when a single rib was taken from him and a woman to attend upon him was supplied in its stead?" (Sanhedrin 39a).

WILLIAM BARCLAY

7

Pride and Prejudice

Women upset everything. When you let them into your life, you find that the woman is driving at one thing and you're driving at another.

GEORGE BERNARD SHAW

Mission Improbable

The man who marries a woman to educate her falls victim to the same fallacy as the woman who marries a man to reform him.

ELBERT HUBBARD

To Laugh or Cry?

In Shakespeare, love is always depicted as comedy – sometimes light and charming, as in *Twelfth Night*, but usually rough and buffoonish, as in *The Taming of the Shrew*. This comic attitude is plainly visible even in such plays as *Hamlet* and *Romeo and Juliet*.

In its main outlines, I suppose, *Hamlet* is properly looked upon as a tragedy, but if you believe that the love passages are intended to be tragic then . . . give a sober reading to the colloquies between Hamlet and Ophelia . . . Shakespeare, through the mouth of Hamlet, derides the whole business with almost intolerable ribaldry.

As for *Romeo and Juliet*, what is it but a penetrating burlesque upon the love guff that was fashionable in the poet's time? True enough, his head buzzed with such loveliness that he could not write even burlesque without making it beautiful – compare *Much Ado About Nothing* and *Othello* – but nevertheless it is still quite absurd to say that he was serious when he wrote this tale of calf love.

Imagine such a man taking seriously the spasms and hallucinations of a flapper of fourteen, the heroics of a boy of

8

eighteen! Shakespeare remembered very well the nature of his own amorous fancies at eighteen. It was the year of his seduction of Anne Hathaway, whose brothers later made him marry her, much to his damage and dismay. He wrote the play at forty-five.

H. L. MENECKEN

4 ~ SOME CURIOSITIES

Love has its curiosities, acclaimed in Books of Records . . .

Unlikely people fall in love – the differences being symbolized in some recorded marriages.

Super-Marriage

The longest marriages on record are for eighty-six years, between Sir Temulji Bhicaji Nariman and Lady Nariman, and another couple – who married in 1743 – Lazarus Rowe and Molly Webber.

Mismatched?

The couple said to have the greatest difference in height between them is Nigel Wilks (6 feet 6 inches) who married Beverley Russell (4 feet) in June 1984.

Two Centuries

The oldest couple to get married is recorded as Harry Stevens (103) and Thelma Lucas (84). They married in the USA in 1984.

Tall Story

The tallest couple to have married is Anna Hanen Swann (7 feet 5½ inches) and Martin Van Buren Bates (7 feet 2½ inches). Their wedding was in London in June 1871.

5 ~ WHAT'S THE ATTRACTION?

A source of speculation, research and debate for centuries is the age-old question as to why one eminently sane and sensible individual suddenly drops all normal habits and falls

11

madly in love with another individual who often – on the face of it – hardly appears to warrant all the devotion and fuss!

Even the garden's common plants exhibit this peculiar phenomenon – take the Convolvulus and the Honeysuckle for example . . .

Attraction of Opposites

The fragrant Honeysuckle spiral clockwise to the sun,
And many other species do the same.
But some climb anti-clockwise: the Bindweed does for
  one –
Or Convolvulus, to give her proper name.

Rooted on either side of the door
One of each species grew,
And twined towards the windowledge above.
Each cork-screwed to the lintel in the only way it
  knew,
Where they stopped, touched tendrils, smiled and fell
  in love.

Said the right-handed-thread Honeysuckle to the
left-handed-thread Bindweed,
"O let us get married, if our parents don't mind,
we'd be happy and caring, we'd be loving and kind,
we'd live happy ever after", said the Honeysuckle to
  the Bindweed.

To the parents it came as a terrible shock.
"The Bindweeds", they cried, "are of inferior stock.
They're uncultivated – of breeding bereft.
We twine to the right and they twine to the left."

FLANDERS AND SWANN

6 ~ FAMILY LIKENESS

You may think you're an adult now, and that your parents no longer influence you . . . don't be too sure of that!

Similar but Opposite

John Cleese:

Falling in love is obviously a great deal more than sexual attraction. And a serious lover is more than a friend you happen to fancy too. But what the extra element is I've no idea. I've never heard it explained. People smile knowingly, say "chemistry", and change the subject. So what is it?

Robin Skynner:

Well I think the reason we're attracted to someone at this very deep level is basically that they are like us – in a psychological sense.

John Cleese:

But the wise saw tells us "opposites attract".

Robin Skynner:

They don't. Or if they do, it's because they seem to be opposites. But what really draws people together is their similarities, and moreover a similarity in one of the most fundamental aspects of all – that of their family backgrounds.

ROBIN SKYNNER AND JOHN CLEESE

7 ~ ENGAGEMENT RING

Traditionally, the course of true love is betrothal and then marriage.

Choosing Love

Psycho-analysis shows that there are deep unconscious motives which contribute to the choice of a love-partner, and

make the two particular people sexually attractive and satis-
factory to each other. The feelings of a man toward a woman
are always influenced by his early attachment to his mother
. . . but . . . this will be more or less unconscious, and may be
very disguised in its manifestations . . . Similar factors are at
work in the woman's choice. Her impressions of her father,
her feelings towards him – admiration, trust, and so on – may
play a predominant part in her choosing a love companion . . .
There are many other factors at work in the complicated
processes that build up a love-relationship or a friendship.
Normal adult relationships always contain fresh elements
which are derived from the new situation – from circumstances
and the personalities of the people we come in contact with,
and from their response to our emotional needs and practical
interests as grown-up people.

MELANIE KLEIN

Third Finger, Left Hand . . . But Why?

Betrothal in early Roman law . . . an essential part of the
ceremony was the giving of the ring, sometimes made of gold,
sometimes, more often, of iron.

The ring was worn on the third finger of the left hand as now
and Aulus Gellius tells why: "The reason for this practice is
that on cutting and opening human bodies . . . it was found
that a very fine nerve proceeded from that finger alone of
which we have spoken, and made its way straight to the
human heart." Since the third finger of the left hand had this
direct connection with the heart it was considered natural to
give it the honour of wearing the engagement ring.

WILLIAM BARCLAY

Two and Two Make . . .

Love and marriage, love and
marriage,
Go together like a horse and carriage.

15

Daft Ditty

> It won't be a stylish marriage,
> I can't afford a carriage;
> But you'll look sweet upon the seat
> Of a bicycle made for two.

The Short-lived Wonder

Of all the misconceptions about love the most powerful and
pervasive is the belief that "falling in love" is love or at least

one of the manifestations of love. It is a potent misconception, because falling in love is subjectively experienced in a very powerful fashion as an experience of love . . . the experience of falling in love is specifically a sex-linked erotic experience . . . (and) is invariably temporary. No matter whom we fall in love with, we sooner or later fall out of love if the relationship continues long enough. This is not to say that we invariably cease loving the person with whom we fell in love. But it is to say that the feeling of ecstatic lovingness that characterizes the experience of falling in love always passes. The honeymoon always ends. The bloom of romance always fades.

M. SCOTT PECK

Handle with Care

Love is like a seed that manages to germinate and poke its head above the ground. But if it doesn't get proper food, light and moisture, it will die. The loving, caring feelings of courtship flower in marriage only if the couple understands that its love needs nurturing every single day. Successful nurturing is related to the process the couple works out between them.

Process refers to the how of marriage. Process consists of the decisions the couple reach together, and the way in which they act on these decisions. I am referring in particular to the kinds of things the two of them have to do together that they once handled alone – such as money, food, work and religion.

Love is the feeling that begins a marriage, but the process is what makes it work.

VIRGINIA SATIR

8 ~ WEDDING BELLS

A public ceremony usually forms an important part of "tying the knot" in marriage.

17

The Act, not the Place, Matters Most

One Saturday morning, licence in hand, we set forth to find some clergyman in some village far from our usual haunts . . . On the point of giving up, we tried a last Rectory; and there we found a white-haired old man who had doubtless been meditating. Perhaps a saint. Thunder rumbled as we went in. He talked to us kindly for a few minutes. Then, as thunder crashed and rain poured down, we were wed. A bedridden sister upstairs signed as witness, which she wasn't; so perhaps it wasn't legal.

As we left, the sun was striking through. The air was rain-washed and cool, and there were bright puddles by the walk. As we drove away, a rainbow appeared. Heaven approved. When we got to the wooded park where we would have a two-day honeymoon – the only guests in a small hotel – we discovered that each of us had a different idea of which village we had finally been married in. In later years, whenever there was some unresolvable difference about a fact, we would chant the names of the two villages at each other . . .

SHELDON VANAUKEN

Fools Rush In

Marriage "must not be undertaken carelessly, lightly or selfishly, but reverently, responsibly and after serious thought . . ."

MARRIAGE SERVICE

Why a Public Ceremony?

There are historic reasons in favour of a public church ceremony. In the Middle Ages it was possible to be validly married in the eyes of the Church privately if a couple promised to take each other as husband and wife and live together as such. These unions were the equivalent of the living together of today, and were called clandestine marriages carried out in private.

18

The same arguments were offered in favour of these alliances as are offered today. The trouble was that these private vows could be and were repudiated. Women found themselves married and abandoned, and men committed themselves privately to more than one woman. The need for public witness became vital.

But these historic reasons are not the only ones. A marriage is both a private commitment and a public event. Society is involved when a couple marry. The couple are no longer free to be courted by anyone else. They gather rights to themselves as married people; they own property and they become the parents of children. In all these areas society is involved in being a public witness to the marriage and also in supporting it in various ways.

Furthermore, Christianity lays great stress on a permanent and exclusive commitment as being proper to marriage. It is only in the presence of a permanent commitment that the couple have the freedom to look at their disappointments, conflicts, differences of opinion without the fear of losing their partners. The vows taken publicly have the strength of reminding the couple when they are at their lowest that they are committed to each other and somehow they have to find an answer to their worst troubles.

JACK DOMINIAN

The Stern Stuff of Commitment

Feelings of being head-over-heels in love with someone are grand and we should enjoy them to the full, but marriages are made of sterner stuff. In the wedding service we are not asked: "Are you in love?" with the other person. We are not even asked: "Do you love?" the other person. We are asked: *"Will you love?"*

Marriage is about our will. It is about making up our minds and promising to keep our word . . . commitment does not end when we stop feeling loving.

GAVIN REID

9 ~ A MARRIAGE IS BORN

Marriages are made in years, not months. They begin when rings are exchanged, and then need years of living to attain maturity.

I Promise You . . .

We promise according to our hopes and perform according to our fears.

FRANÇOIS, DUC DE LA ROCHEFOUCAULD

The Wedding Present

A wedding is *not* a marriage. A wedding is only the beginning of an undertaking that may or may not, someday, develop into a marriage. What the couple have on their wedding day is not the key to a beautiful garden but just a vacant lot and a few gardening tools.

DAVID AND VERA MACE

End to Means

We had the experience but missed the meaning.

T. S. ELIOT

You Stop and I Begin

There is something amphibious about marriage, something neither fish nor fowl. It is like a three-legged sack race or a cloth-covered dancing horse, except that it is not only the feet and body but one's whole being that gets tangled up in the other person's. Marriage is not just a sharing but a mingling of identities, a consanguinity of psyches. It is a blend so intimate that it actually becomes hard to tell where one person leaves off and another begins.

MIKE MASON

Transforming

The flower must be transformed in order to become a fruit. The fruit must be transformed in order to become a seed. The seed must be transformed in order to become a living, thriving tree. If you would love, you must be transformed, for through the commitment involved in love you enter upon a new life. You will no longer see, feel, act, understand, or even pray in the same way. Yours is a shared life now, a life enriched through sharing with the other. Through your daily gift of life, you become mutually fruitful, not merely biologically but at every level of your make-up. You are born anew so that you may be slowly *re-created*. Consequently genuine love is indissoluble.

MICHEL QUOIST

PART TWO

A Marriage Is . . .

1 ~ TWO HEARTS AS ONE

Married love is (or should be) a union of lives and a fusion of hearts.

Union

Marriage is not a federation of two sovereign states.
It is a union –

domestic
social
spiritual
physical.
It is a fusion of two hearts –

the union of two lives –
the coming together of two tributaries,
which, after being joined in marriage, will flow
in the same channel
in the same direction . . .
carrying the same burdens of responsibility and
obligation.

PETER MARSHALL

Stickable

The "glue" that holds a marriage together is supplied by the ability of each partner to meet the needs of the other . . .

JIM CONWAY

Two Into Three

Motherhood is not an isolated relationship; for some people . . . it may seem so, but it has always sprung out of a relationship with a man. A woman comes to being a mother out of a whole background of living and loving that places her maternity in context. For me that context was, and always will be, Peter.

When we married we always knew we would want to have children, but for the first few years we wanted to be alone. Even the most discreet baby would have deprived us of the joy of relaxed aloneness together. It was a joy that seemed endless at the time, although we knew that slowly, imperceptibly we would move towards that point at which we could say with spontaneous sincerity, "Now we are ready to have a child". That was exactly how it happened . . . Suddenly we were both aware that we now felt ready for them; our love had had space and freedom in which to uncoil and to stretch, to become aware of itself, and at last was ready to move into a new phase.

What was it that we wanted in wanting children? We wanted to share our love, to bring other human beings into the light and warmth of an existence that was founded on love, to give something of what we had received, of the joy that we felt almost too guilty to relish alone . . . We would be co-operators with God in creation, privileged to contribute to the new world with flesh of our flesh, love of our love, life of our life . . .

MARGARET HEBBLETHWAITE

Seal of Commitment

. . . the first purpose of sex is the ending of isolation and loneliness. And loneliness can only end where trust exists – trust that someone has made a commitment to me and I to that person in a sworn covenant until death parts us. Within such a relationship the physical pleasures of sex may blossom and mysteriously deepen to solidify the relationship . . . We marry to make an alliance of mutual help and service and as an expression of love. Intimacy in such a context is the seal of commitment. It is also a delicate communication of love and trust by which a man and a woman know each other ever more deeply.

JOHN WHITE

25

2 ~ A SHARED COMMITMENT

In marriage we look for intimacy within the security of commit-ment.

Good Not Bad

Pleasure is God's invention and not the devil's.

C. S. LEWIS

Needed – Closeness

A man needs to have an intimate relationship with other people. He needs to have at least one person with whom he can be open. He needs to share what he really is – his joys and anxieties. Most people expect that marriage will provide that kind of intimacy.

JIM CONWAY

Playing in Harmony

All deep and authentic friendships, and especially the union of those who are married, must be based on absolute openness and honesty. At times, gut-level communication will be most difficult, but it is at these precise times that it is most necessary. Among close friends or between partners in marriage there will come from time to time a complete emotional and personal communion.

In our human condition this can never be a permanent experience. There should and will be, however, moments when encounter attains perfect communication. At these times the two persons will feel an almost perfect and mutual empathy. I know that my own reactions are shared completely

by my friend; my happiness or my grief is perfectly redupli-
cated in him. We are like two musical instruments playing
exactly the same note, filled with and giving forth precisely the
same sound.

JOHN POWELL

Spiritual Fun

Erotic love-making is not meant to be an austere, conscience-
searching spiritual exercise. It can be spiritual. But it can also
be fun.

JOHN WHITE

It's A Pleasure

C. S. Lewis . . . distinguishes *need-pleasures* that focus on the
individual who has the pleasure and what it does for him (the
thirsty man's "I need that glass of water"), and *appreciative-
pleasures* which focus on the object of pleasure (the connois-
seur's "That wine was marvellous").

Venus, or sexual desire, is a need-pleasure in which the
other is a means to satisfy my desire; Eros, or being in love, is
an appreciative-pleasure in which I desire a woman for herself,
not because she is a woman (for any woman can satisfy the
need for sex). I do not desire her as a means for satisfying my
sexual desire. Indeed sexual desire is not paramount and may
not come first in time.

TONY WALTER

3 ~ TENDER LOVING CARE

Commitment to care for one's partner for life is one of the
attributes of a really good marriage – one to be treasured or
coveted.

Arms Around Each Other

There is the old story about a farm couple who learned how to signal each other when they needed encouragement. If the man needed TLC (tender loving care), he would walk into the kitchen and toss his hat on the table. This was a signal to his wife that she needed to encourage and strengthen him. If the

husband came in from the field and saw his wife wearing her apron backwards, this was a sign that he needed to bear some of her burdens.

One day, the inevitable happened. He walked in from the field and threw his hat on the table – and she had her apron on backwards. When a couple has been practising encouraging and supporting one another – even when they both need help at the same time – they can, in the midst of their need, put their arms around each other and cry together, each receiving strength from the other.

JIM CONWAY

The Queen Mother

After Edward VIII abdicated from the throne to marry Mrs Simpson, "Bertie" and Elizabeth – the Duke and Duchess of York – became king and queen.

Even the outgoing king, in his famous farewell radio broadcast from Windsor Castle, had acknowledged the advantages Elizabeth conferred on his brother. "He has one matchless blessing, enjoyed by so many of you and not bestowed on me – a happy home with his wife and children."

The new king, for his part, paid tribute to his consort on his first full day as monarch, addressing a loyal if shell-shocked gathering of his Privy Council: "With my wife and helpmeet by my side, I take up the heavy burden which lies before me." His wife and helpmeet, if truth be known, was equally appalled by the "awful" fate which had befallen them . . .

At first the new king was unable to conceal from his intimates the full extent of his bewilderment. He passed from a state of shock through one of numbness to sheer emotional exhaustion. But with the help of his single-minded wife, he soon began to tap reserves of strength which perhaps only such a crisis could have revealed . . .

ANTHONY HOLDEN

Mary Whitehouse

A journalist once said to Mary Whitehouse: "You must have a remarkable marriage for it to be able to stand up to a strain like this."

"I do. I have a remarkable husband, too, who in his quiet self-effacing way has always been so ready to sacrifice his ease and comfort and to advise and support.

"For instance, who does all the shopping and planning ahead of meals? Certainly not me. Who thinks about the money I shall need when I set out on a journey? Not me either! Who prays for the family, for the work, for me when I'm too exhausted to do anything but put my head on the pillow and fall asleep? Ernest."

MARY WHITEHOUSE

4 ~ LOVE IS A SPENDTHRIFT

Married love is like being joined as two hands in prayer and like two hands who give of themselves generously.

Love rarely balances the books. It is generous in its giving, and unafraid to go into the red.

In Or Out

Love is not gazing at each other, but a looking outward together, in the same direction.

THOMAS HARRIS

Shining Armour

When the medieval knight engaged in a tournament for the
sake of his lady, the victory which he sought to win over his
opponent was meant to be an outward and visible sign, as we
might put it, of his utter self-giving to her . . .

W. NORMAN PITTINGER

Me Last!

When my desire for the health and wellbeing of another person becomes equal to my desire for my own health and wellbeing, then a state of love exists.

HARRY STACK SULLIVAN

Extravagance

Love is a spendthrift, leaves its arithmetic at home, is always "in the red" . . .

P. SCHERER

Joined As Two Hands In Prayer

You can find many couples making their way through life arm in arm, for physical union is relatively easy to attain. You will find far fewer who have achieved a union of hearts, for it is relatively difficult to love someone else with tenderness. Rarely you will encounter true spiritual union, for few are married in the spirit. Marriage in the spirit demands that you share all through a mutual confidence – all your ideas, your expressions, your needs, your doubts, your regrets, your plans, your dreams, your joys, your disappointments . . . all that comprises the inner world of the spirit. Marriage in the spirit leads you – through mutual give-and-take – to a common attitude of love toward your brothers and your God. Marriage in the spirit – through an ever-deepening knowledge of one another – brings you together before God, joined as two hands in prayer. Don't try to deceive the other or yourself. See yourself as you really are, don't hesitate to reveal yourself to the other. It is only through mutual candour that you will become one. If you remain in the shadows of secrecy, you will never love. You must reveal to the other what lies behind external appearances.

MICHEL QUOIST

5 ~ A PARTNER IS A PERSON

For a happy marriage value your partner as a cherished person, and never use your partner as an object.

I Love You For Being You

To love another as an object is to love him as a "thing", as a commodity which can be used, exploited or enjoyed and then cast off. But to love another person we must begin by granting him his own autonomy and identity as a person. We have to love him for what he is in himself, and not for what he is to us. We have to love him for his own good, not for the good we get out of him. And this is impossible unless we are capable of a love which "transforms" us, so to speak, into the other person, making us able to see things as he sees them, love what he loves, experience the deeper realities of his own life as if they were our own.

THOMAS MERTON

Family Business

During courtship neither person is yet sure of the other, but each tries to win the other. Both are alive, attractive, interesting, even beautiful – inasmuch as aliveness always makes the face beautiful. Neither yet *has* the other; hence each one's energy is directed to *being*, i.e. to giving to and stimulating the other.

With the act of marriage the situation frequently changes fundamentally. The marriage contract gives each partner the exclusive possession of the other's body, feelings and care. Nobody has to be won over any more, because love has become something one *has*, a property.

33

The two cease to make the effort to be lovable and to produce love, hence they become boring, and hence their beauty disappears. They are disappointed and puzzled. Are they not the same persons any more? Did they make a mistake in the first place? Each usually seeks the cause of the change in the other and feels defrauded. What they do not see is that they no longer are the same people they were when they were in love with each other; that the error that one can *have* love led them to cease loving.

Now instead of settling for loving each other, they settle for owning together what they have: money, social standing, a home, children. Thus, in some cases, the marriage initiated on the basis of love becomes transformed into a friendly ownership, a corporation in which two egotisms are pooled into one: that of the family.

ERICH FROMM

Law of Life

It is a law of human life, as certain as gravity: To live fully, we must learn to *use* things and *love* people . . . not *love* things and *use* people.

JOHN POWELL

Doing Not Owning

Can one *have* love? If we could, love would need to be a thing, a substance that one can have, own, possess. The truth is, there is no such thing as "love". "Love" is an abstraction . . . In reality, there exists only the *act of loving*. To love is a productive activity. It implies a caring for, knowing, responding, affirming, enjoying: the person, the tree, the painting, the idea. It means bringing to life, increasing his/her/its aliveness. It is a process, self-renewing and self-increasing.

When love is experienced in the mode of having it implies confining, imprisoning, or controlling the object one "loves". It is strangling, deadening, suffocating, killing, not life-giving.

What people call *love* is mostly a misuse of the word, in order to hide the reality of their not loving . . .

ERICH FROMM

6 ~ DREAMING, DARING AND TAKING RISKS

Dreaming great dreams, running big risks, and daring to work for the impossible, all feature in the richness of much married love.

Questioning Dreamers

To love itself is a dangerous game. The risks are formidable, yet the rewards are beyond price. We dare only what we can dare, and we may need help to dare more, in life and in bed.

First we must know what we want; we must know ourselves. Only thus may we be our own person, truly free to make the most of the new world we face and the new choices it may offer us.

If we deny that rich heritage which we may call our emotions or our spirit or the questioning dreamer within, the world will be a bleaker space.

PRUDENCE TUNNADINE

The Cost is Courage

As soon as a husband and wife have the courage to be completely open with one another, whatever the cost, their marriage becomes once more a wonderful adventure.

PAUL TOURNIER

35

Virginia Woolf

Did her marriage bear on her writing or was it peripheral? It is obvious that Leonard Woolf propped the outer structure of her career: he established a press to publish her works; he kept unwanted visitors at bay; he read final drafts and made just comments. But did he affect that self that his wife reserved for her work? . . .

. . . Virginia Woolf's marriage was crucial to her, not so much for the practical reason of Leonard's protection nor for the literary reason that he provided, as did her parents, subject-matter for her work, but because marriage itself presented a complementary challenge to becoming an artist: to be creative in private life . . .

. . . "No woman was ever nearer to her mate than I am", Jane Eyre concludes. ". . . We talk, I believe, all day long." Virginia and Leonard Woolf first discovered their compatibility in this way . . . he noticed how "the spring of a fantastic imagination" seemed to bubble up "from strange recesses". It made him catch his breath as on a mountain when suddenly the wind blows. Her mind appeared "so astonishingly fearless" that it made his pulses beat. There was no fact that she would not frankly touch. It made life seem to go quickly, and at the same time, it made him feel protective. He thought: "I am always frightened that with her eyes fixed on the great rocks she will stumble among the stones." . . .

Before their engagement they had forged a private language that both created and preserved their secret world. During the course of their marriage her thoughts, whenever she was away, seem to have homed in on Leonard and she would hasten back to their delicious discourse . . .

Ten years after the (mental) breakdown in which she would not see Leonard, she claimed him as the hidden core of her life and the source of her freshness . . . Divine contentment, not tame nursing shaped the authorial character who came into being in the spring of 1925 when she conceived her two greatest books . . . LYNDALL GORDON

Mrs Beeton's Marriage Recipe

Isabella Beeton's decision to write for Sam of course transformed the nature of their marital relationship and in due
course had an equally fundamental effect on his business . . .
she ceased to occupy the traditional role of the dependent wife
and turned her marriage into one of the most fruitful professional partnerships of the time.

37

She was a fully fledged working wife in the modern sense in all respects but one – that she could not earn money of her own. That she should be entitled to almost certainly never entered her head; the fact that she represented an inestimable financial bargain never occurred to Sam either in crude terms, although he was extremely conscious of the extent and value of her work, and referred to her more than once, in a very humble spirit, as his "master" . . .

She died, aged 28, following childbirth . . . unknown to the world at her death. No one could possibly have foreseen that her name would be revived and that in due course Sam . . . would be eclipsed by her fame . . .

She was a woman who succeeded in a man's world without sacrificing any of the femininity they so highly prized – on the contrary, her success, paradoxically, was a consequence of it, for her career was her husband's creation; had it not been for him, the legendary Mrs Beeton would never have been.

SARAH FREEMAN

7 ~ TWO BRANCHES ON ONE TREE

A good marriage is the union of a man and a woman who still cherish their individuality.

Apart In Togetherness

The genuine lover always perceives the beloved as someone who has a totally separate identity. (He) always respects and even encourages this separateness and the unique individuality of the beloved. Failure to perceive and respect this separateness is extremely common . . .

Not too long ago, in a couples' group, I heard one of the members state that the "purpose and function" of his wife was to keep their house neat and him well fed. I was aghast at what seemed to me his painfully blatant male chauvinism . . . to my horror the six others, male and female alike, gave very similar answers. All of them defined the purpose and function of their husbands or wives in reference to themselves; all of them failed to perceive that their mates might have an existence basically separate from their own or any kind of destiny apart from their marriage.

"Good grief," I exclaimed, "it's no wonder that you are all having difficulties in your marriages, and you'll continue to have difficulties until you come to recognize that each of you has your own separate destiny to fulfil." The group felt not only chastised but profoundly confused by my pronouncement.

Somewhat belligerently they asked me to define the purpose and function of my wife. "The purpose and function of Lily", I responded, "is to grow and be the most of which she is capable, not for my benefit but for her own and for the glory of God." . . .

Great marriages cannot be constructed by individuals who are terrified by their basic aloneness, as so commonly is the case, and seek a merging in marriage. Genuine love not only respects the individuality of the other but actually seeks to cultivate it, even at the risk of separation and loss. The ultimate goal of life remains the spiritual growth of the individual, the solitary journey to peaks that can be climbed only alone. Significant journeys cannot be accomplished without the nurture provided by a successful marriage or a successful society.

M. SCOTT PECK

Separate Love

Love is a powerful feeling that releases the potential of one person to strive for his dreams without threat of judgement, to momentarily transcend his need for the need of another, to be patient and not to lose his feeling of worth as the struggle to find meaning with the other person occurs, as bridges between individual differentnesses are built, and while he bears the loneliness that inevitably exists from time to time when each person must, in order to live his own integrity, take separate ways from the other.

VIRGINIA SATIR

Make Way

A good marriage is that in which each appoints the other guardian of his solitude.

RAINER MARIA RILKE

Tolkien

Writing of his wife Edith, Ronald Tolkien says: "Her hair was raven, her skin clear, her eyes bright, and she could sing – and dance."

She sang and danced for him in the wood, and from this came the story that was to be the centre of *The Silmarillion*: the tale of the mortal man Beren who loves the immortal elven-maiden Luthien Tinuviel, whom he first sees dancing among hemlock in a wood . . . This deeply romantic fairy-story encompasses a wider range of emotions than anything Tolkien had previously written, achieving at times a Wagnerian intensity of passion . . .

After Edith's death more than fifty years later he wrote to his son Christopher, explaining . . . "She was (and knew she was) my Luthien . . ."

To some extent Ronald and Edith lived separate lives . . . sleeping in different bedrooms and keeping different hours. He worked late, partly because he was short of time in the day, and also because it was not until she had gone to bed that he could stay at his desk without interruption . . . These frequent interruptions, themselves no more than an understandable demand from Edith for affection and attention, were often an irritant to him though he bore them patiently.

Yet it would be wrong to picture her as excluded totally from his work. During these years he did not share his writing with her anything like as fully as he had done . . . and although she was not well acquainted with the details of his books and did not have a deep understanding of them, he did not shut her out from this side of his life . . .

HUMPHREY CARPENTER

Dodie Smith

(Playwright, author of *The Hundred and One Dalmatians* . . .)

. . . whenever practical we have continued to prefer separate bedrooms. I am quite sure this has contributed to the long happiness of our marriage. We spend so much more time together than the average married couple, sharing so many of our waking hours. We are always so happy in each other's company and yet we both of us like a certain amount of privacy. The nights are a good time for it.

Possibly we are freaks, though perfectly normal regarding sexual matters. And as we have now been happily married for over forty-five years, I sometimes think many marriages might benefit from our kind of freakishness . . .

DODIE SMITH

Room For Space

But let there be spaces in your togetherness,
And let the winds of the heavens dance between you.
Love one another, but make not a bond of love:
Let it rather be a moving sea between the shores of
    your souls.
Fill each other's cup but drink not from one cup.
Give one another of your bread but eat not from the
    same loaf.

41

Sing and dance together and be joyous, but let each of
   you be alone,
Even as the strings of a lute are alone though they
   quiver with the same music.
Give your hearts, but not into each other's keeping.
For only the hand of Life can contain your hearts.
And stand together yet not too near together;
For the pillars of the temple stand apart,
And the oak tree and the cypress grow not in each
   other's shadow.

KAHLIL GIBRAN

8 ~ MARRIAGE IS FUN!

Marriage is more than solemnity and commitment. Making time to have fun is also important.

Survival Kit Clowns

"Fun" is another big word in our marriage relationship. I reckon that a sense of humour is often a manifestation of the image of God in us . . . both partners need to be able to let their hair down, do some clowning, enjoy a bit of whole-hearted irresponsibility. Fun based on a sharing of the adult and the child in each of us is a wholesome and necessary part of the survival kit – often ignored by those who are addicted to being bossy without the leaven of humour. Children and grand-children should provide a wonderful opportunity and re-minder that the child in each of us is treasured by God and is holy.

JIM THOMPSON
(Bishop of Stepney)

9 ~ GROWING TOGETHER

Within the safety of securely belonging to another person, the marriage partners can begin to experiment and to grow to individual maturity.

43

Heart At Home

Someone has observed: "Familiarity breeds comfort and comfort is like bread – necessary and nourishing, but taken for granted and unexciting." . . . This facet of love we call *belonging* is essential to your happiness in marriage.

We all need a place we can call home – not just bricks and mortar and four walls, but an atmosphere that is secure, where we feel completely comfortable with each other in the sureness that we belong, and that our happiness and well-being are of the utmost importance to our partner.

John Powell has captured the essence of this love in one sentence: "We need the heart of another as a home for our hearts."

ED WHEAT

Understand

I think a man and a woman should choose each other for life, for the simple reason that a long life is barely enough for a man and woman to understand each other; and to understand is to love.

J. B. YEATS

Ring of Confidence

Marriages may grow, or fail to grow, depending on whether the husband and wife develop a greater trust in each other, a greater confidence in themselves . . .

MASTERS AND JOHNSON

Pointer

As iron sharpens iron, so one person sharpens another.

PROVERBS 27:17

The Growth Factor

God has designed the human personality with a great potential for growth. If both people in the marriage are growing,
there should never come a time when they know all that there
is to know about each other. Their relationship will remain
fresh, and there won't be the likelihood of boredom.

JIM CONWAY

10 ~ NEW DISCOVERIES OR DANGER AHEAD!

The time comes when the thrill of discovering new things
fades – for almost all is now known about the partner.

Reality seems dull and disappointing. The excitement of
discovery departs.

Daily fights or poisonous silences may express underlying
emotions which corrode the relationship, or these emotions
may be used to weld a relationship which weathers life's
storms.

Discoveries

Courtship's beautiful curiosity has been lost. The thirst for
discovery and for understanding has dried up. The husband
believes that now he does understand his wife. At the first
word from her lips he makes a little sign of exasperation which
means, "You're telling me the same old story!" In the face of
such a reaction how can the other dare to express herself? Yet,
the less she expresses herself, the less she will be understood;
the less she feels understood, the more she will withdraw into

herself. The thrill of discovery has been lost. If you think you know your wife or husband, it is because you have given up any real attempt to discover him. The difference between the image you have made of him, and what he really is, will ever grow deeper.

PAUL TOURNIER

Smashing the Beauty

Have you ever tried to describe a whole panorama of mountains as they look when the air is crystal clear and the sun has just set, colouring them all rosy pink, while the sky turns powder blue and the full moon slithers up behind the peaks to add its breathtaking copper sphere to the other beauty? Have you tried to describe this during fog and slashing rain when even the trees across the fields cannot be seen? . . .

Adultery is the smashing of a rare and beautiful thing, a unity, a oneness between two people who have become one because of something which God has made them to be capable of having together, which had the original purpose of making two people one.

EDITH SHAEFFER

Four Bare Legs in Bed

When I was a youngster, all the progressive people were saying, "Why all this prudery? Let us treat sex just as we treat all our other impulses." I was simple-minded enough to believe they meant what they said.

I have since discovered that they meant exactly the opposite. They meant that sex was to be treated as no other impulse in our nature has ever been treated by civilized people.

All the others, we admit, have to be bridled . . . But every unkindness and breach of faith seems to be condoned, provided that the object aimed at is "four bare legs in bed".

It is like having a morality in which stealing fruit is considered wrong – unless you steal nectarines.

C. S. LEWIS

Dripping

A quarrelsome wife is like a constant dripping on a rainy day;
restraining her is like restraining the wind or grasping oil with
the hand.

PROVERBS 27:15–16

Abraham and Mary Lincoln

Abraham Lincoln has been the subject of so much myth-
making that we cannot separate truth from fiction in the story
of his marriage . . . (which) caused almost as much gossip as
the engagement . . . we must conclude that a great deal of
nonsense has been written about Mrs Lincoln.

She was subject to fits of temper which passed the bounds of
eccentricity. On the other hand she was a gently reared
woman, married to one of the most untidy, careless, uncon-
ventional and moody of men.

Lincoln could never make himself look like other men, or
make a room which he had inhabited for a few hours look like
other rooms. Disorder and physical confusion attended him
like shadows. And although it is a virtue to think deeply,
prolonged and impenetrable silences in the home do not make
for married ease.

Lincoln seems to have been mildly sardonic towards the
niceties, the sense of social dignity, which his wife brought
with her from Kentucky. Asked about the spelling of her
family name, he replied: "One 'd' is enough for God, but the
Todds must have two!" And he once praised a long-trained
dress, of which Mary Lincoln was proud, by walking around
her and exclaiming: "Phew! What a long tail our coat has!"

HERBERT AGAR

Fight For Life

Couples who fight together are couples who stay together –
provided they know how to fight properly!

ANONYMOUS

47

Wedding Riot

The Blue Dolphin Restaurant in San Leandro, California, has been the scene of numerous memorable gatherings, but none perhaps quite so unforgettable as the wedding reception that took place in mid-June.

As the three hundred guests chatted happily among themselves, they suddenly grew silent when the newly-weds began arguing in loud voices. Dismay turned to disbelief when the groom grabbed the wedding cake and threw it in his bride's face.

By the time the police squad pulled up, guests were breaking chairs and smashing mirrors. It took half an hour for more than thirty police to get the crowd under control.

By that time the newly-weds had disappeared.

ANONYMOUS REPORTER

11 ~ "I'M SORRY . . ."

Forgiveness of oneself and for one's partner can be the secret source of strength, enabling a marriage to survive.

Left Alone

O Lord, we pray for those who, full of confidence and love, once chose a partner for life, and are now alone after final separation. May they receive the gift of time, so that hurt and bitterness may be redeemed by healing and love, personal weakness by your strength, inner despair by the joy of knowing you and serving others; through Jesus Christ our Lord.

SUSAN WILLIAMS

Seven To Three

Marriage is three parts love and seven parts forgiveness.

LANGDON MITCHELL

Know

(He) illustrates, not the doubtful maxim that to know all is to forgive all, but the unshakeable truth that to forgive is to know. He who loves, sees.

C. S. LEWIS

Bear

You can bear your own faults, and why not a fault in your wife?

BENJAMIN FRANKLIN

Pity

> The humblest and the happiest pair
> Will find occasion to forbear;
> And something, every day they live
> To pity, and perhaps forgive.

WILLIAM COWPER

Divorce Your Dream

It's never too late to really "marry" the one who shares bed and board with you. You only have to make up your mind to do it. Three is a crowd: your wife, yourself and your dream. If you really want to get married, divorce your dream. If you can't build a castle you can at least build a hut, but you'll never be happy in your hut if you're still dreaming of living in a castle. Let's assume that you've made up your mind to break with your dream, to abandon your hopes for a castle . . . Is this then the end of your illusions? No, this determination of itself will not be sufficient to dispel them once and for all. You will have to start by *forgiving* the other, for you have never forgiven your husband or wife for not being equal to your dream. Offer your disappointments to God, offer him your shattered dreams, your dissatisfaction, your rancour, your discouragement. Finally, accept the real person whom you have married, and your life together as it *really* is. It's not a question of remaking your world but of remaking your own attitudes.

MICHEL QUOIST

Back To Basics

The basis of mutual forgiveness is not that the other person is worthy of being forgiven, nor do we forgive because we ourselves have an especially generous nature. The basic principle is that God has forgiven us and, therefore, we are *obligated* to forgive each other. In fact, whenever we repeat the Lord's Prayer, we are saying to God, "Forgive me to the same degree that I am willing to forgive someone else."

JIM CONWAY

PART THREE

The Later Years

Some marriages turn to silver.
Mid-life is typically
a time of stress and of growth for
marriages. It is celebrated at
the Silver Wedding.

1 ~ REBUILD THE FIRE

Marriage . . .
    a small flame springs to life,
    tinsel mellows into gold,
    and the unique, exotic experience of
married love still remains, at times,
an enormous inconvenience!

Coaxing Embers To Life

If renewal in a marriage is to come about, however, there must
be time when a couple can be alone to rekindle the dying fire.

It's not enough to say, "Too bad, the fire is going out". You
need time to rebuild the fire. New pieces of wood need to be
added; the old coals need to be stirred; and probably you will

need to get down on your hands and knees and blow on the embers. But finally a small flame leaps up through the new wood, and you can begin to enjoy the warmth and fascination of the fire.

JIM CONWAY

Tinsel Transmuted To Gold

We are standing within arm's reach of that which is most humanly rewarding and beautiful. We must not turn back now. We can still share all the things we once shared with such excitement, when first I told you who I was and you told me who you were; only now our sharing will be deeper because we are deeper.

If I will continue to hear you with the same sense of wonder and joy as I did in the beginning, and you will hear me in this way, our friendship will grow firmer and deeper roots.

54

The tinsel of our first sharing will mellow into gold. We can and will be sure that there is no need to hide anything from each other, that we have shared everything.

JOHN POWELL

Tree Of Marriage

A marriage, or a marriage partner, may be compared to a great tree growing right up through the centre of one's living room.

It is something that is just there, and it is huge, and everything has been built around it, and wherever one happens to be going – to the fridge, to bed, to the bathroom, or out the front door – the tree has to be taken into account. It cannot be gone through; it must respectfully be gone around.

It is somehow bigger and stronger than oneself. True, it could be chopped down, but not without tearing the house apart. And certainly it is beautiful, unique, exotic: but let's face it, it is at times an enormous inconvenience.

MIKE MASON

Shelved

At a time when the woman needs to feel not just a dear old soul but irresistible, her man feels the same. She is miserable and temperamental, wondering what will become of her now her children are gone perhaps, and she feels it is their turn to be sexy and fertile now.

Can she retrain, become a professional grandmother? Few can be surgeons or prime ministers. And in her physical state she barely has the zip for a coffee-morning or a day's washing.

He too, his job promotions now unlikely, his sons beating him at games, needs the reassurance that he still has the young lion in him. He is dangerously more likely to find it from the young girl at the office who, incidentally, sees him as an exciting authority figure and not slumped with his slippers and cocoa over "Match of the Day".

PRUDENCE TUNNADINE

55

Companions

Middle age presents many couples with the opportunity for true companionship, for by now it is clear that shared interests and a healthy respect for privacy are not mutually exclusive.

There is a good chance of having someone to grow old with, to share friends and memories and walks in the rain with, someone to absorb the hush of a household where children no longer reside and to make it resonate with the noise of recaptured joys together.

GAIL SHEEHY

Silver Wedding

Love seems the swiftest, but it is the slowest of all growths. No man or woman knows what perfect love is until they have been married a quarter of a century.

MARK TWAIN

Consumer Satisfaction

Studies record a dramatic climb in satisfaction with marriage in the mid-forties for those couples who have survived the passage into mid-life together. What this finding reflects is not that our mate miraculously improves but that our tolerance can become spontaneous once we stop displacing our inner contradictions on our spouse.

GAIL SHEEHY

2 ~ FROM SILVER TO GOLD

Some marriages move from silver to gold, when what was precious goes through testing and emerges glowing like gold.

Duet To Duel

A marriage is a lot like our house. While new it sparkles. Fresh smells, fun surprises and new discoveries make each day snap, crackle and pop. Of course there's work to be done, but the newness takes away the hassle. As time passes, however, things change. Slowly, almost imperceptibly, the grit of responsibility, mixed with the grind of routine, starts to take its toll. Who hasn't experienced it?

Bills become due. Weeds sprout. Doors squeak and sag. Windows stick. Paint peels. Roofs leak. Taps drip. Drains clog. Floors lose their lustre. The fun and games silently erode into relentless, demanding, irritating tasks. The dreams fade into the misty memories of "the way we were", introducing us into nightmarish and fearful feelings of "the way it is".

The warm, passionate fire that once cast a spell upon us is obviously dying down. Thoughts and words once foreign to us now reside in our heads and tumble out of our mouths. Suddenly we realize we're faced with a decision: move or stay and decorate. Walk away from the embers or rekindle the fire . . . the duet has become a duel . . . the magic is gone.

CHARLES SWINDOLL

The Miracle Of A Second Chance

Writing of her second husband, Rab Butler (Former Chancellor of the Exchequer, Home Secretary, Chairman of the Conservative Party, and Master of Trinity College, Cambridge . . .) whom she married when she was 55, Mollie Butler says:

I was given a miracle . . . he and I turned towards each other for mutual comfort, and in doing so found a depth of devotion that was to last the rest of our lives. Much is written about young love but love in middle life is like a renaissance and is as strong as anything I have ever known.

They had both nursed their previous partners through distressing illnesses. After Rab died she wrote that she had come to see that:

I was not a miserable and lonely creature, but how jolly lucky I had been. That being loved well was rather like being a camel, that one could store it and live on it long after the men had gone.

MOLLIE BUTLER

3 ~ UNITED IN DEATH

Death divides even the closest of partners – but they, of all people, are the most likely to believe in reunion in the after-life.

Sybil Thorndike

At the celebrations of her ninetieth birthday . . . I asked her if she had any real regrets:

"Not many: sometimes I wish I didn't have such a temper, and I wish Lewis [her late husband] and I hadn't had to quarrel so dreadfully, but then again I think that was so much a part of us and our marriage that we couldn't have lived in any other way.

"My mother gave me a great zest for life, and my father made me know how important it was to love God and people, but they were a jolly strong and noisy couple and I don't think I could ever have lived what you might call a quiet life . . .

"I find I dream a lot more than I used to, usually about a place near the sea where there are great rocks and there's a stretch of sand: whenever I have that dream Lewis is always standing there, so I hope perhaps that's where we're going in another life."

SYBIL THORNDIKE

Margaret Rutherford

After a fifteen-year courtship it seemed logical for the lovers to get married. Margaret was fifty-three, Stringer forty-six . . .

Getting out of the train one night she found Stringer standing on the platform.

They walked arm-in-arm back to Margaret's home where, right in the hallway before she even had time to put down her handbag, Stringer fell on one knee (she thought of the dashing Errol Flynn as Sir Walter Raleigh and herself as Elizabeth I) and rather poetically proposed. "Wilt thou have this man to be thy wedded husband . . . for better or worse, for richer for poorer, in sickness and in health?"

"Of course," she replied, rising to the occasion, "I would marry you even if you lived in a Bedouin tent." . . .

Remembering (Stringer) Robert Morley says: "I don't think I can subscribe to your view that Stringer sacrificed his career for Margaret. Unkind critics (of which, I fear, I was one) found his devotion and protection too good to be true, but on reflection I think I misjudged him as he certainly died of a broken heart once she was gone."

DAWN LANGLEY SIMMONDS
AND ARTHUR BAKER

In Her Full And Good Reality

. . . as I have discovered, passionate grief does not link us with the dead but cuts us off from them. This becomes clearer and clearer. It is just at those moments when I feel least sorrow – getting into my morning bath is one of them – that H. rushes upon my mind in her full reality, her otherness. Not, as in my worst moments, all foreshortened and patheticized and solemnized by miseries, but as she is in her own right. This is good and tonic.

C. S. LEWIS

Marie Curie

After Pierre Curie was killed by a large cart, the body, still in its wretched condition, was brought by ambulance to the house two hours later . . . It was laid out in a room on the ground floor. There she had to suffer the sight of the wreck of a man who had given her all the years of her life that mattered. Whatever stress they had had to suffer together can now only have seemed of unutterably minimal importance.

Pierre Curie had given her both the love of their early years and the access to a life she could otherwise never have known. What was left of that dream they had planned was now at its end, but the part they had succeeded in living out together had been truly shared.

Curie had never taken so much as a tiny fraction more of this share of credit than had been his due. She, who could so easily have had to take second place when the honours were doled out, never did so as a result of any of his actions or wishes. His generosity had ensured her equal acknowledgement for equal achievement. The suffering too, both physical and mental, had been equally borne.

ROBERT REID

Living Dead

As Disraeli lay dying he heard that Queen Victoria was proposing to visit him. His response was: "Why should I see her? She will only want me to give a message to Albert."

When Kindness Killed

It seemed that the old Browns belonged for ever, and that the miracle of their survival was made commonplace by the durability of their love – if one could call it love, such a balance. Then suddenly, within the space of two days, feebleness took them both. It was as though two machines, wound up and synchronized, had run down at exactly the same time. Their interdependence was so legendary we didn't notice their plight at first. But after a week, not having been seen about, some neighbours thought it best to call. They found old Hannah on the kitchen floor feeding her man with a spoon. He was lying in a corner half-covered with matting, and they were both too weak to stand . . .

Well, the Authorities were told: the Visiting Spinsters got busy; and it was decided they would have to be moved. They were too frail to help each other now, their children were too scattered, too busy. There was but one thing to be done; it was for the best; they would have to be moved to the Workhouse.

The old couple were shocked and terrified, and lay clutching each other's hands. "The Workhouse" – always a word of shame, grey shadow falling on the close of life . . . Hannah and Joseph thanked the Visiting Spinsters but pleaded to be left at home, to be left as they wanted, to cause no trouble, just simply to stay together. The Workhouse could not give them the mercy they needed, but could only divide them in charity. Much better to hide, or die in a ditch, or to starve in one's familiar kitchen, watched by the objects one's life had gathered . . .

"You'll be well looked after," the Spinsters said, "and you'll see each other twice a week." The bright busy voices cajoled with authority and the old couple were not trained to defy them. So that same afternoon, white and speechless, they were taken away to the Workhouse. Hannah Brown was put to bed in the Women's Wing, and Joseph lay in the Men's. It was the first time, in all their fifty years, that they had ever been separated. They did not see each other again, for in a week they both were dead.

LAURIE LEE

The New World

They that love beyond the world cannot be separated. Death cannot kill what never dies. Death is but crossing the world as friends do the seas: they live in one another still.

WILLIAM PENN

4 ~ IN MEMORIAM

The understatements used in writings about those who have died, often reveal a rich quality of loving coveted by others . . .

Blessing Beloved

Warm summer sun shine kindly here:
Warm summer wind blow softly here:
Green sod above lie light, lie light:
Good-night, Dear Heart: good-night, good-night.

Memorial to Clorinda Haywood,
St Bartholomew's, Edgbaston

Love's Nevers

But true love is a durable fire,
In the mind ever burning,
Never sick, never old, never dead,
From itself never turning.

SIR WALTER RALEGH

Without You

He first deceas'd; she for a little tried
To live without him:
Lik'd it not, and died.

SIR HENRY WOTTON

Love's Last Knot

To these, whom Death again did wed,
This grave's their second marriage-bed.
For though the hand of fate could force
'Twixt soul and body a divorce,
It could not sunder man and wife,
'Cause they both lived but one life.
Peace, good Reader. Do not weep.
Peace, the lovers are asleep.
They, sweet turtles, folded lie
In the last knot love could tie;
And though they lie as they were dead,
Their pillow stone, their sheets of lead
(Pillow hard, and sheets not warm)
Love made the bed; they'll take not harm.
Let them sleep: let them sleep on,
Till this stormy night be gone,
Till the eternal morrow dawn;
Then the curtains will be drawn
And they wake into a light
Whose day shall never die in night.

CRASHAW

Roman Relic

This was Eusebia, brothers, a rare and most chaste wife who spent with me a life of marriage, as time tells: sixty years, eight months and twenty days. God himself was pleased with her life, as I say. Truly a gentle wife of the rarest sort: I, Sexus Successus, lawyer, her husband, beg that you always remember her in your prayers, brothers.

From The Museum, Kairouan, Tunisia

List of Wedding Anniversaries

1   Cotton (or paper)
2   Paper (or cotton)
3   Leather
4   Silk (or flowers)
5   Wood
6   Sugar (or iron)
7   Wool (or copper)
8   Bronze
9   Pottery
10   Tin
11   Steel
12   Silk and fine linen
13   Lace
14   Ivory
15   Crystal
20   China
25   Silver
30   Pearl
35   Coral
40   Ruby
45   Sapphire
50   Golden
55   Emerald
60   Diamond

Notes

PART ONE

1 *Joyce Grenfell Requests the Pleasure*, Macmillan 1986, p. 90
  To Have or To Be, Abacus, p. 52

2 Quoted by Helmuth Thielicke, *The Ethics of Sex*, James Clarke
  1978, p. 136
  The Power and Meaning of Love, Sheldon Press, pp. 29–30
  The Marriage Encounter, Bantam Books, New York 1975, p. 119
  Some Fruits of Solitude, 1693
  Code poem used by Violette Szabo, the British Resistance heroine
  who worked in France and was shot at Ravensbruck
  Concentration Camp.

3 *All You Love is Need*, SPCK 1985, p. 60
  Strike the Original Match, Kingsway 1983, p. 60
  The Third Wave, Collins 1980, p. 235
  The Plain Man's Guide to Ethics, Fount Paperbacks, pp. 107–8
  Pygmalion, 1913
  The Note Book, 1927
  Selected Prejudices, Jonathan Cape (Traveller's Library series) 1928, p. 110

4 *Guinness Book of Records*, 1987

5 *At the Drop of a Hat*, 1957

6 *Families and How to Survive Them*, Methuen 1983, p. 16

7 *Love, Guilt and Reparation*, Virago, p. 324
  The Plain Man's Guide to Ethics, Fount Paperbacks, pp. 127–8
  The Road Less Travelled, Rider, pp. 84–5
  Peoplemaking, Souvenir Press 1972, p. 128

8 *A Severe Mercy*, Hodder & Stoughton 1977, pp. 47–8, 164–5, 175–6
The Marriage Service, Church of England, *Alternative Service Book*
The Growth of Love and Sex, Darton, Longman & Todd 1982
Starting Out Together, Hodder & Stoughton 1984, p. 12

9 Quoted in *Long Term Marriage*, Thatcher, Hodder & Stoughton 1980, p. 25
The Mystery of Marriage, MARC Europe 1987, p. 131
The Christian Response, Gill & Macmillan, p. 119

PART TWO

1 Quoted by his widow, Catherine Marshall, in *A Man Called Peter*, Fount Paperbacks, pp. 62–3
Men in Mid-life Crisis, Paternoster Press 1980, p. 119
Motherhood and God, Geoffrey Chapman 1984, pp. 13–14
Eros Defiled, InterVarsity Press 1983, p. 16

2 Quoted in *Eros Defiled* by John White, IVP 1983, p. 14
Men in Mid-Life Crisis, Paternoster Press 1983, p. 117
Why Am I Afraid to Tell You Who I Am?, Fontana 1960, pp. 61–2
Eros Defiled, IVP 1983, p. 24
All You Love is Need, SPCK 1985, p. 68

3 *Men in Mid-life Crisis*, Paternoster Press 1980, p. 126
The Queen Mother, Sphere Books 1985, pp. 79ff
A Most Dangerous Woman, Lion Publishing 1982, p. 33

4 *The Christian Response*, Gill & Macmillan, p. 116
Love Looks Deep, Mowbray 1969
Quoted by David and Vera Mace, in *Love and Anger in Marriage*, Marshall Pickering 1983, p. 53
Love Is A Spendthrift, New York, Harper Brothers 1961
I'm OK – You're OK, Harper & Row, p. 143

5 *The Power and Meaning of Love*, Sheldon Press, pp. 7–8
To Have or To Be, Abacus, p. 53
Why Am I Afraid to Tell You Who I Am?, Fontana 1975, p. 134
To Have or To Be, Abacus, p. 52

6 *The Making of Love*, Unwin 1985, p. 220
The Adventure of Living, Highland Books 1983

Virginia Woolf – A Writer's Life, Oxford University Press 1986, pp. 132, 140, 141, 146, 159
Isabella and Sam – the story of Mrs Beeton, Gollancz 1977, pp. 134, 237

7 *The Road Less Travelled*, Rider, pp. 161, 166, 168
Peoplemaking, Souvenir Press 1972, p. 124
Letters, 1892–1910; 1910–26
J. R. R. Tolkien – a biography, George Allen & Unwin 1977, pp. 97, 157
The Prophet, Penguin Books
Look Back With Gratitude, Muller, Blond and White Ltd 1985, p. 4

8 *Half Way*, Fount 1986, p. 60

9 *Love Life for Every Married Couple*, Marshall Pickering 1984, p. 98
Quoted by Ed Wheat in *Love Life for Every Married Couple*, Marshall Pickering 1984, p. 112
The Pleasure Bond, Boston: Little Brown and Co. 1974, p. 37
Men in Mid-life Crisis, Paternoster Press 1980, p. 119

10 *Marriage Difficulties*, Highland Books, p. 14
Lifelines, Hodder & Stoughton, p. 143
God In the Dock, Fount Paperbacks 1979, pp. 105–6
Abraham Lincoln, Collins 1958
The Britannica Book of the Year, 1980. The section "Unusual but Noteworthy events" is quoted in David and Vera Mace, *Love and Anger in Marriage*, Marshall Pickering 1983, p. 9

11 Tony Castle, *The Hodder Book of Christian Prayers*, Hodder & Stoughton 1986, p. 213
The New York Idea, 1907
Introduction to *George MacDonald: An Anthology*, Fount Paperbacks 1983, p. xxiv
Poor Richard's Almanack (1732–57)
The Christian Response, Gill & Macmillan, p. 121
Men in Mid-life Crisis, Paternoster Press 1980, p. 124

PART THREE

1 *Men in Mid-life Crisis*, Paternoster Press 1980, p. 121
Why Am I Afraid To Tell You Who I Am?, Fontana 1975, p. 101
The Mystery of Marriage, MARC Europe 1987, p. 31

The Making of Love, Unwin 1985, p. 218
Passages, Bantam 1980, p. 506
Notebook, 1935
Passages, Bantam 1980, p. 506

2 *Strike the Original Match*, Kingsway Publications 1983, p. 10
   August and Rab, Weidenfeld and Nicolson 1987 (from an interview in *The Times* 28 August 1987)

3 Sheridan Morley, *A Life In The Theatre*, Weidenfeld & Nicolson 1977, p. 143
   Margaret Rutherford – A Blithe Spirit, Dawn Langley Simmonds and Arthur Baker, Weidenfeld 1983, pp. 63–4, 184
   A Grief Observed, Faber & Faber 1961
   Marie Curie, Collins 1974, pp. 149–50
   Cider with Rosie, Hogarth Press

4 *Oxford Book of Death*, p. 320
   "As you came from the Holy Land", *Oxford Book of Death*, p. 269
   "Upon the Death of Sir Albert Morton's Wife", *Oxford Book of Death*, p. 250
   "An Epitaph upon a Young Married Couple, Dead and Buried Together", *Oxford Book of Death*, p. 248